Recorded Insights

Tarot Reader's Log

The Celtic Cross Tarot
Readings and Predictions

By Pitisci

Tarot Reader's Log - A diagrammatic journal of your Tarot readings and predictions Copyright © 2018 by Vincent Pitisci

All rights reserved. No part of this book may be reproduced in any form, except brief excerpts for purpose of review without written permission from the author.

Dedication

To all of those wishing to learn the Tarot

Sharing my thoughts on how I use the log book:

How a log will help you:
In order to improve on any subject we need to be able to measure our progress. The practice of reading the Tarot seems to just lightly skim over that aspect of our journey. Like many other types of study, one sure-fire way of keeping track of what you've done so far, is to keep it on record. This allows us to go back and see where we are now as opposed to where we were yesterday. A measure of your progress and what caused you to progress.

The advantage of this approach:
Ultimately we want to learn how to interpret the cards correctly. Accurately. Logging your readings allows us to go back and look at our readings once events have come to pass. This enables us to see the same cards, only now in the present. Can we see what came to pass in those same cards now? What did we miss? Do we see it now that it has happened? Looking at our readings in the present allows us to see and interpret what actually did come to pass. This sharpens our insight for future readings. It allows us to see what happened in the cards that we initially laid down when the event was still to come. It allows us to see, in the cards, what actually did happen. Doing so enables us to sharpen our insight of what the cards can show us in future readings.

We can see it in black and white right in front of us. By going back and viewing our cards in the present we can improve our insight for seeing the cards for the future. Knowing what has happened and forcing yourself to see it in those same cards expands your ability with the Tarot.

The importance of a complete and consistent card spread.
Just like a chess master will play her games on a consistent playing field of 64 squares of a chess board, I feel it is beneficial to use the same card spread for every reading you do. In order to do that you need to be using a card spread that will find useful answers to any question asked of it. Four basic elements in your card spread will do that. They are WHAT, WHY, HOW and WHEN. If your card spread covers those elements in the reading you have a good card spread. The way I use the Celtic Cross does cover those vital elements. Shown in this chapter is the position meanings of my Celtic Cross. I feel those elements used cover those four basic aspects of any question very well. It is time tested as I have used this method of the Celtic Cross professionally for over 25 years and I have never seen a question I couldn't answer using it!

The actual logging section of this book:
You have a total of 63 blank two-page spreads in this book to record 63 readings on. These 63 two-page spreads are divided into three sections. Section 1, Section 2, and Section 3 making it convenient to use. In the beginning you will find a Directory of those three Sections as well. This allows you to easily file your readings so you can relocate them again at a later date. Each of the 63 two page spreads has a ghost image of a blank Celtic Cross on one page allowing you to jot down what cards were played in the reading.

The positions are not numbered or assigned any meanings allowing you to use the pattern any way you choose to use it. The other page is used for notes on your reading. If you like my Celtic Cross method I cover it in many YouTubes and in my books as well. But the basics is shown right here for you and that's all you need to get the idea.

More on the Log Book:

Just write the card drawn in each position in the diagram page...Queen of Cups in position #1, 9 of Swords in position #2 and so on. Later, you can confirm and check what was seen and what was overlooked. What was missed? Using this journal will allow you to see future readings with more scope and not miss a trick in what the cards are telling you. This type of resource will sharpen your vision with the Tarot cards as time passes. The journal allows you to record 63 readings to be viewed and analyzed again and again.

Recording your readings can be a useful application to keep track of details seen in specific readings you have done. It will allow you to see your predictions as they come to pass and fine tune your interpretations of the cards as you saw them when the reading was initially done.

It allows you to confirm prediction in a black and white page of what you saw. It also allows you to view the reading once the "prediction" has gone through time.

What you saw a month ago can now be recorded and the insight can be seen clearly once the event or circumstance has occurred. Were you accurate? Can you now see the elements that you missed when the reading was done?

Recording the reading allows you to see it in the present once time has past and identify the actual things that occurred. Can you see them in the cards now that things have happened?

The advantage of a consistent procedure in your card reading is immeasurable. Just like the chess master has consistency in using a chess board to create art in her game of chess. 64 consistent squares for every game played allows the chess master millions of unique insightful possibilities into each game played.

A consistent card spread that can answer any question asked of it is valuable to a good reader. Over the years of my deep experience with the Tarot I have created a profound level Celtic Cross that will do just that. You are more than welcome to use it with this journal or use your own version of this classic Tarot card spread.

Your scratches of cards don't have to be as neat as a pin. As long as you understand what you wrote it's fine. Here are some suggestions I use when I record cards to paper.
- The Six of Wanda............6/wands
- The High Priestess ......HP
- The Hanged Man ....H Man
* The Ten of Pentacles 10/coins
- The Magician ....Magi
- Temperance .....Temp
- The Queen of Swords ... Qu/swords
- The Knight of Cups ....Knight/cups

You get the idea!

Celtic Cross 2.0

The Slanted Cross – A new look at an old map

A look into WHAT – WHY – HOW – WHEN

Positions #1, #2 & #7 .... A look at WHAT is the reason for this question.

These three positions allows us to look deep into the question itself and how clearly the client sees the situation.

Positions #3, #4 & #9 .... A look at WHY they want this in their life.

These three positions allows us to look deep into why they want this in their life and the actions they're taking to achieve this goal. Are the efforts being made the correct ones to take? We can question the real purpose of the question here and the efforts being taken by the client at this time.

Positions #5, #6 & #10 .... A look at HOW are they going to achieve this goal.

These three positions allows us to look deep into ways of finding solutions to succeed. To find opportunities to watch for and to get a glimps at results that can be expected. A prediction.

Position #8 .... The timing – WHEN. Is it time to act before opportunities are lost? Or time to wait for a more advantagous time when things are more in your favor for the best outcome..

Celtic Cross 2.0

The Slanted Cross – A new look at an old map

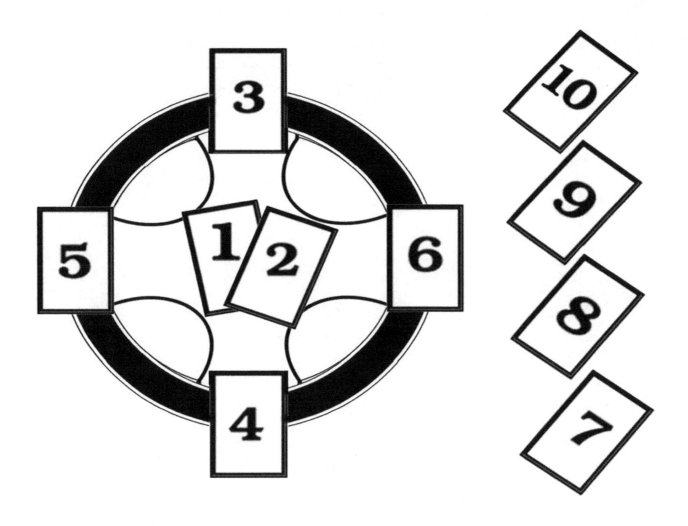

Celtic Cross 2.0
The Slanted Cross – A new look at an old map

Shown on the following page is the way I do the Celtic Cross. After 25 years of using the Cross this way on a professional basis I can safely say it is a time tested and useful method of this classic card spread. It can answer any question asked and therefore the only spread you will ever need.

`~ Vincent Pitisci

Celtic Cross

#3
What actions the client is currently taking and are they the best actions to take?

#10
A prediction based on actions to be taken. Also, finer details of things to watch for – good and bad.

#9
The purpose of this goal. A look at the bigger picture.

#5
An asset the client has that will help achieve the goal sought

#1

#2
These two positions together represent the question itself. Can the question be rephrased?

#6
An opportunity to come the client needs to watch for

#8
The timing is key. Is it time to act? Or do we wait for a more favorable time.

#4
What the client's immediate goals are from the actions taken from pos #3?

#7
Client's viewpoint of their own question. Is it correct?

Your Directory of your readings

Section #1 Pages 16 thru 56

Page 16. _____

Page 18. _____

Page 20. _____

Page 22. _____

Page 24. _____

Page 26. _____

Page 28. _____

Page 30. _____

Page 32. _____

Page 34. _____

Page 36. _____

Page 38. _____

Page 40. _____

Page 42. _____

Page 44. _____

Page 46. _____

Page 48. _____

Page 50. _____

Page 52. _____

Page 54. _____

Page 56. _____

Section #2 Pages 60 thru 100

Page 60. _____

Page 62. _____

Page 64. _____

Page 66. _____

Page 68. _____

Page 70. _____

Page 72. _____

Page 74. _____

Page 76. _____

Page 78. _____

Page 80. _____

Page 82. _____

Page 84. _____

Page 86. _____

Page 88. _____

Page 90. _____

Page 92. _____

Page 94. _____

Page 96. _____

Page 98. _____

Page 100. _____

Section #3 Pages 104 thru 144

Page 104. _____

Page 106. _____

Page 108. _____

Page 110. _____

Page 112. _____

Page 114. _____

Page 116. _____

Page 118. _____

Page 120. _____

Page 122. _____

Page 124. _____

Page 126. _____

Page 128. _____

Page 130. _____

Page 132. _____

Page 134. _____

Page 136. _____

Page 138. _____

Page 140. _____

Page 142. _____

Page 144. _____

Section #1

The Seeker _____   Date._____

The Question :

Key notes :

Closure & Predictions:

The Seeker _____   Date._____

The Question :

Key notes :

Closure & Predictions:

The Seeker _____   Date._____

The Question :

Key notes :

Closure & Predictions:

The Seeker _____ Date._____

The Question :

Key notes :

Closure & Predictions:

The Seeker _____   Date._____

The Question :

Key notes :

Closure & Predictions:

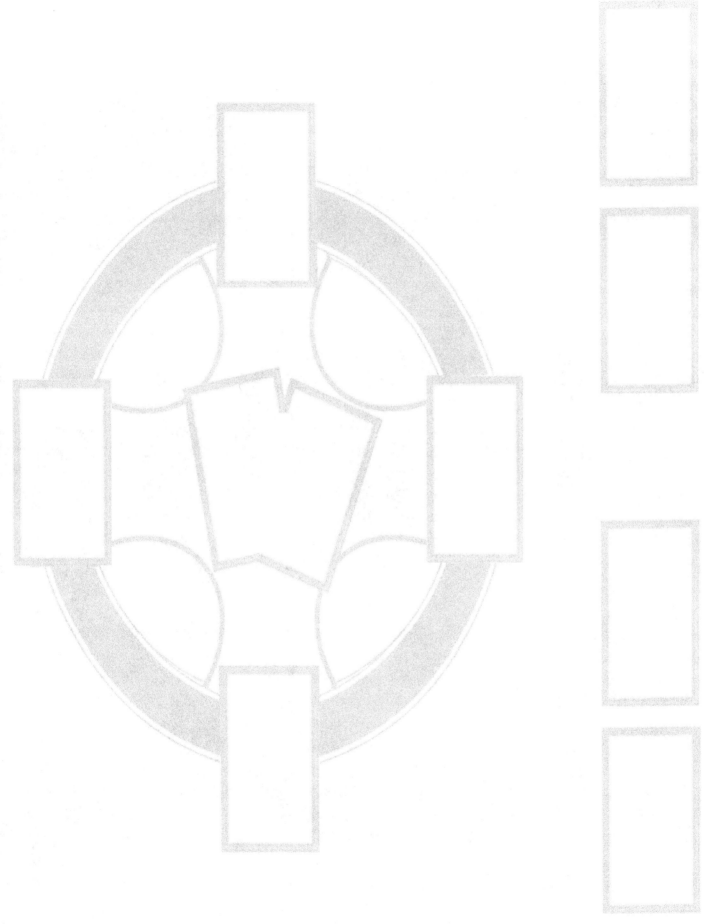

The Seeker _____   Date._____

The Question :

Key notes :

Closure & Predictions:

The Seeker _____   Date._____

The Question :

Key notes :

Closure & Predictions:

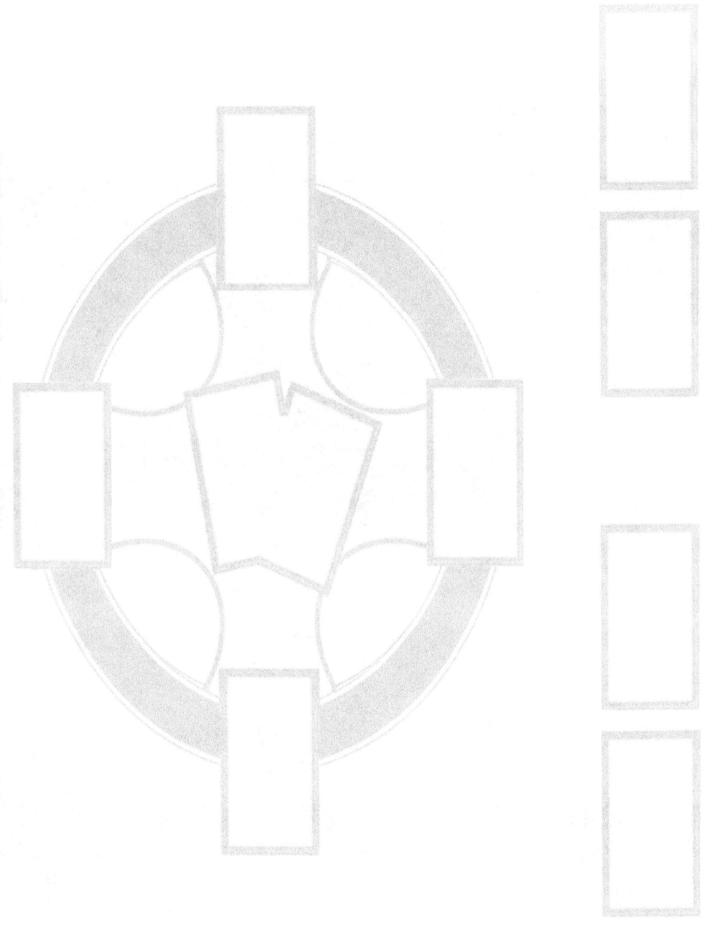

The Seeker _____ Date._____

The Question :

Key notes :

Closure & Predictions:

The Seeker _____   Date._____

The Question :

Key notes :

Closure & Predictions:

The Seeker _____ Date._____

The Question :

Key notes :

Closure & Predictions:

The Seeker _____   Date._____

The Question :

Key notes :

Closure & Predictions:

The Seeker _____   Date._____

The Question :

Key notes :

Closure & Predictions:

The Seeker _____   Date._____

The Question :

Key notes :

Closure & Predictions:

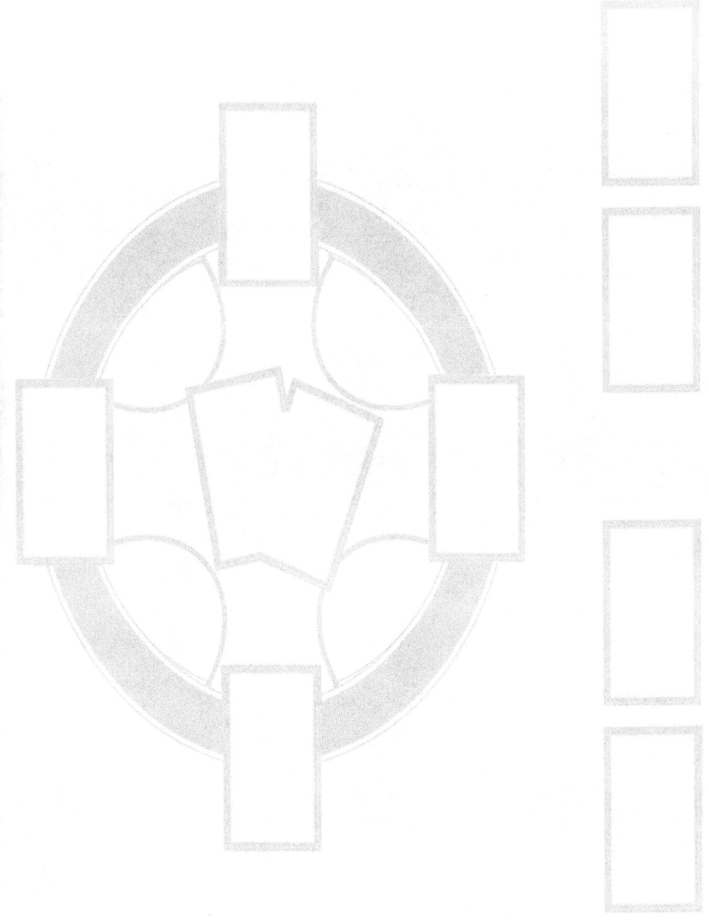

The Seeker _____   Date._____

The Question :

Key notes :

Closure & Predictions:

The Seeker _____   Date._____

The Question :

Key notes :

Closure & Predictions:

The Seeker _____   Date._____

The Question :

Key notes :

Closure & Predictions:

The Seeker _____   Date._____

The Question :

Key notes :

Closure & Predictions:

The Seeker _____ Date._____

The Question :

Key notes :

Closure & Predictions:

The Seeker _____   Date._____

The Question :

Key notes :

Closure & Predictions:

The Seeker _____   Date._____

The Question :

Key notes :

Closure & Predictions:

The Seeker _____ Date._____

The Question :

Key notes :

Closure & Predictions:

Section #2

The Seeker _____   Date._____

The Question :

Key notes :

Closure & Predictions:

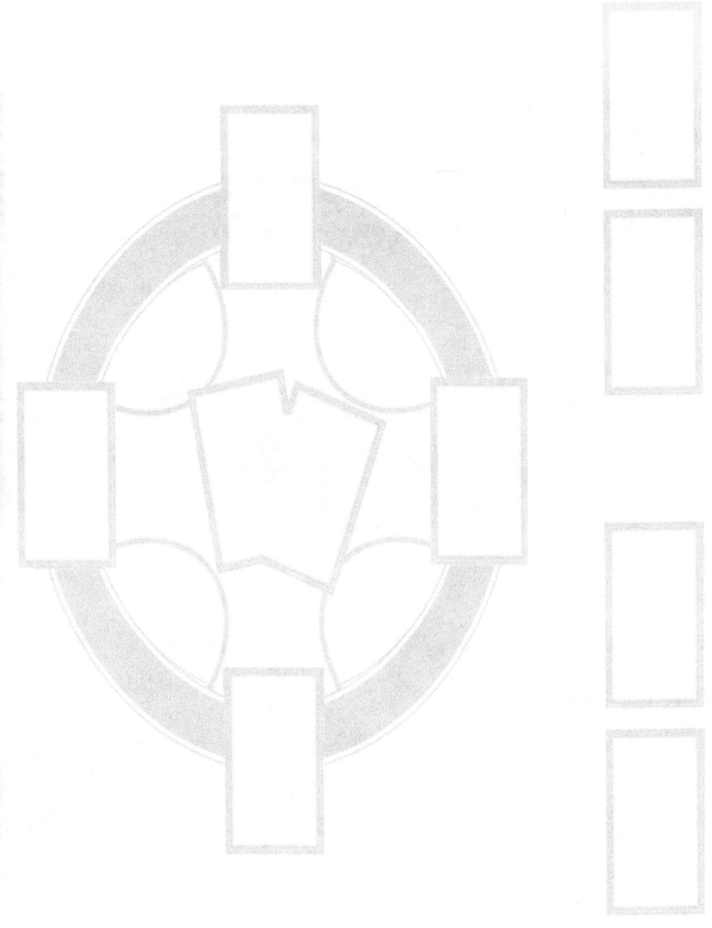

The Seeker _____   Date._____

The Question :

Key notes :

Closure & Predictions:

The Seeker _____   Date._____

The Question :

Key notes :

Closure & Predictions:

The Seeker _____   Date._____

The Question :

Key notes :

Closure & Predictions:

The Seeker _____   Date._____

The Question :

Key notes :

Closure & Predictions:

The Seeker _____   Date._____

The Question :

Key notes :

Closure & Predictions:

The Seeker _____   Date._____

The Question :

Key notes :

Closure & Predictions:

The Seeker _____   Date._____

The Question :

Key notes :

Closure & Predictions:

The Seeker _____   Date._____

The Question :

Key notes :

Closure & Predictions:

The Seeker _____ Date._____

The Question :

Key notes :

Closure & Predictions:

The Seeker _____   Date._____

The Question :

Key notes :

Closure & Predictions:

The Seeker _____		Date._____

The Question :

Key notes :

Closure & Predictions:

The Seeker _____   Date._____

The Question :

Key notes :

Closure & Predictions:

The Seeker _____   Date._____

The Question :

Key notes :

Closure & Predictions:

The Seeker _____   Date._____

The Question :

Key notes :

Closure & Predictions:

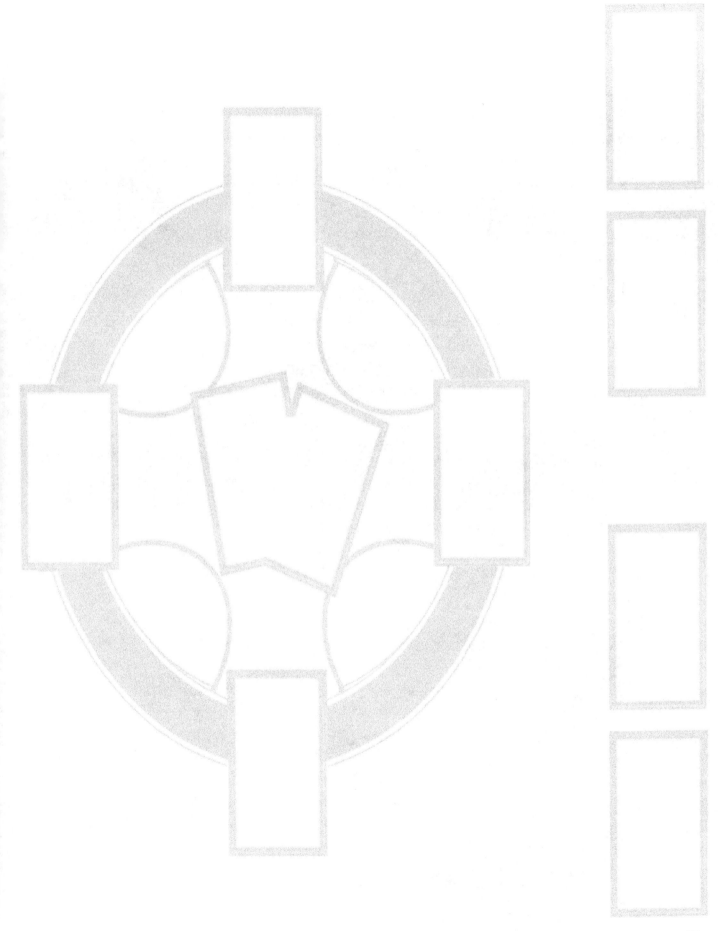

The Seeker _____   Date._____

The Question :

Key notes :

Closure & Predictions:

The Seeker _____   Date._____

The Question :

Key notes :

Closure & Predictions:

The Seeker _____   Date._____

The Question :

Key notes :

Closure & Predictions:

The Seeker _____ Date._____

The Question :

Key notes :

Closure & Predictions:

The Seeker _____   Date._____

The Question :

Key notes :

Closure & Predictions:

The Seeker _____   Date._____

The Question :

Key notes :

Closure & Predictions:

Section #3

The Seeker _____		Date._____

The Question :

Key notes :

Closure & Predictions:

The Seeker _____   Date._____

The Question :

Key notes :

Closure & Predictions:

The Seeker _____ Date._____

The Question :

Key notes :

Closure & Predictions:

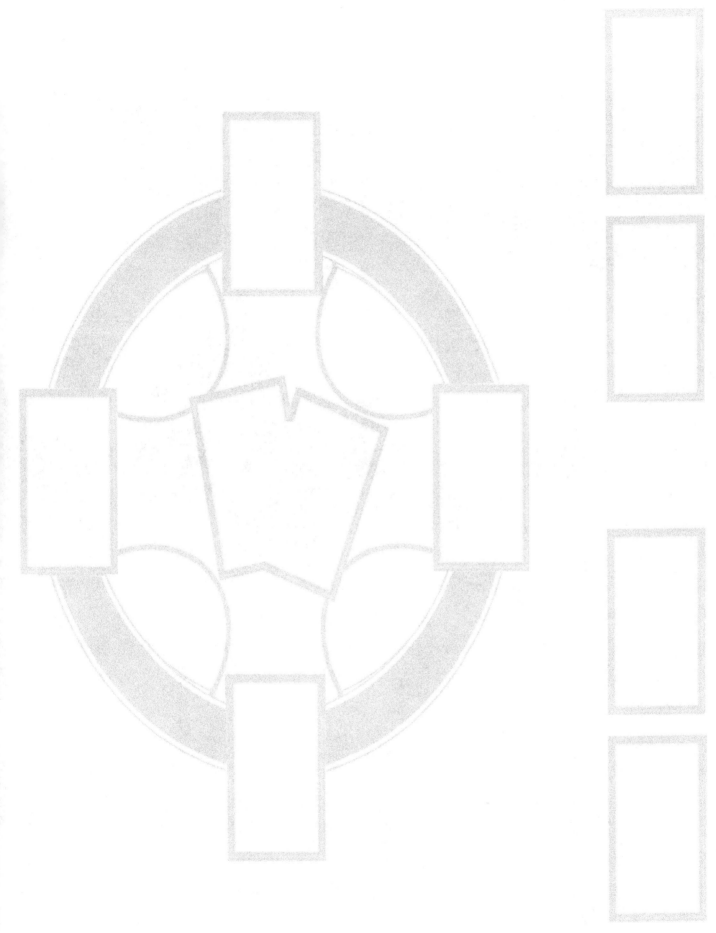

The Seeker _____   Date._____

The Question :

Key notes :

Closure & Predictions:

The Seeker _____ Date._____

The Question :

Key notes :

Closure & Predictions:

The Seeker _____   Date._____

The Question :

Key notes :

Closure & Predictions:

The Seeker _____   Date._____

The Question :

Key notes :

Closure & Predictions:

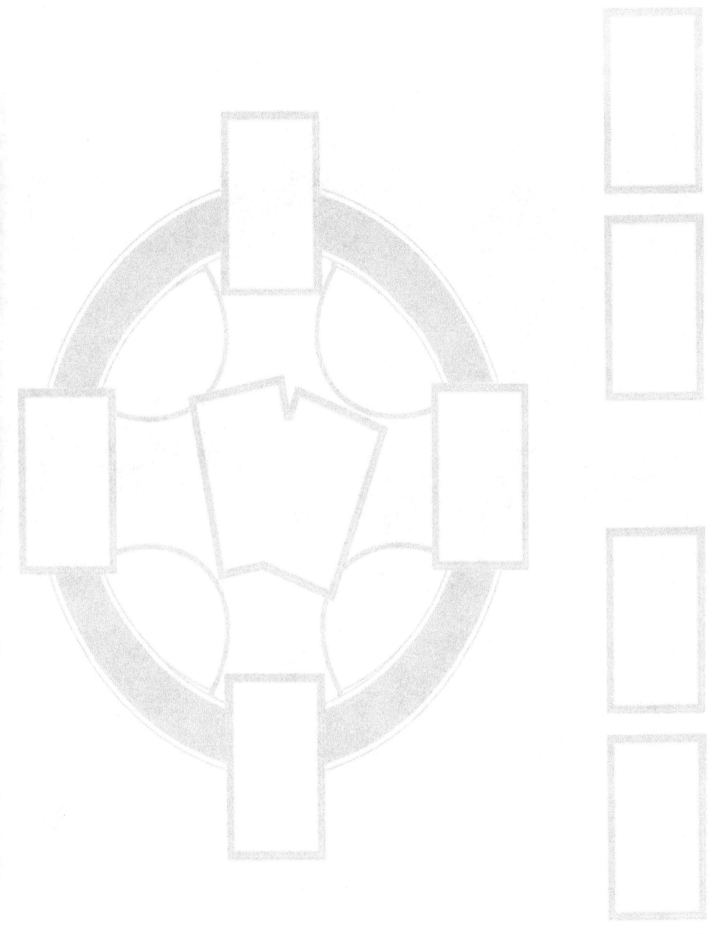

The Seeker _____   Date._____

The Question :

Key notes :

Closure & Predictions:

The Seeker _____   Date._____

The Question :

Key notes :

Closure & Predictions:

The Seeker _____ Date._____

The Question :

Key notes :

Closure & Predictions:

The Seeker _____   Date._____

The Question :

Key notes :

Closure & Predictions:

The Seeker _____   Date._____

The Question :

Key notes :

Closure & Predictions:

The Seeker _____ Date._____

The Question :

Key notes :

Closure & Predictions:

The Seeker _____ Date._____

The Question :

Key notes :

Closure & Predictions:

The Seeker _____   Date._____

The Question :

Key notes :

Closure & Predictions:

The Seeker _____ Date._____

The Question :

Key notes :

Closure & Predictions:

The Seeker _____ Date._____

The Question :

Key notes :

Closure & Predictions:

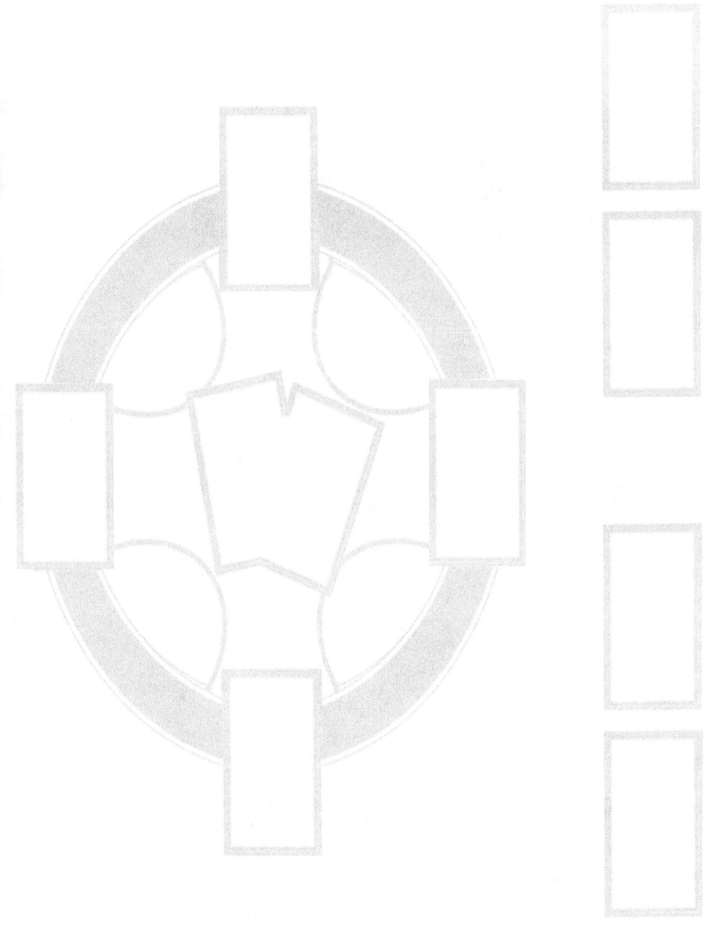

The Seeker _____ Date._____

The Question :

Key notes :

Closure & Predictions:

The Seeker _____ Date._____

The Question :

Key notes :

Closure & Predictions:

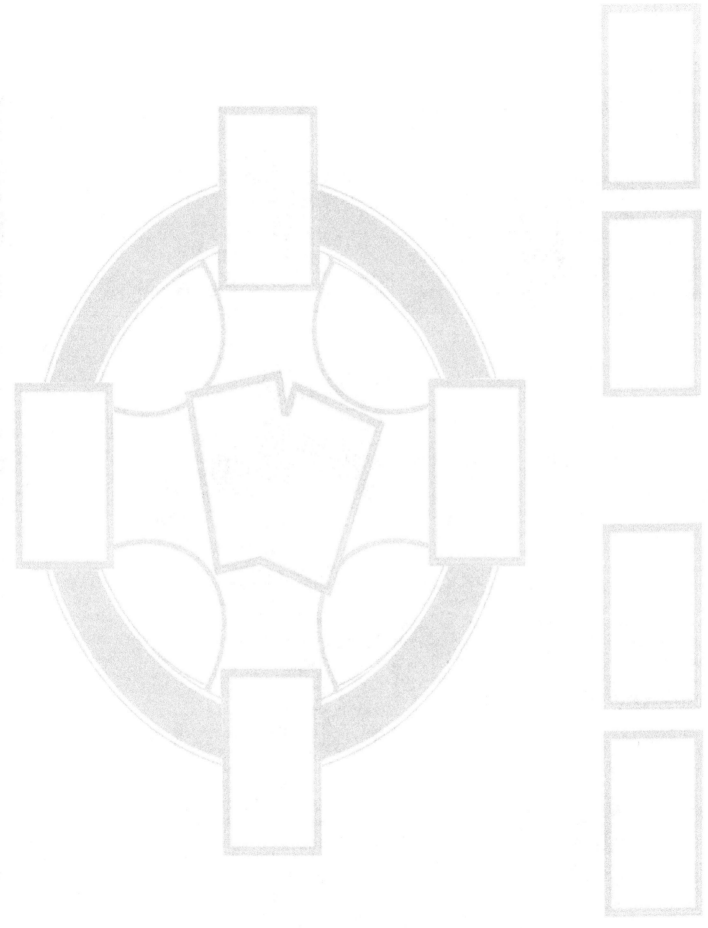

The Seeker _____   Date._____

The Question :

Key notes :

Closure & Predictions:

The Seeker _____   Date._____

The Question :

Key notes :

Closure & Predictions:

CPSIA information can be obtained
at www.ICGtesting.com
Printed in the USA
LVHW101001270119
605399LV00037B/948/P